LIVES OF THE
SLEEPERS

THE ERNEST SANDEEN PRIZE IN POETRY

LIVES OF THE
SLEEPERS

NED BALBO

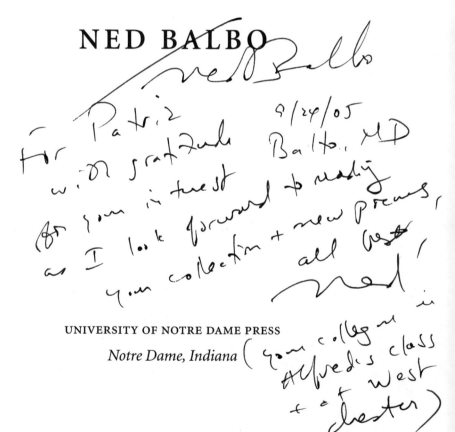

For Patris
with gratitude
for your interest
as I look forward to reading
your collection + new poems,
all best,
Ned

9/24/05
Balto., MD

(your colleague in
Alfred's class
+ of West
chester)

UNIVERSITY OF NOTRE DAME PRESS
Notre Dame, Indiana

Library of Congress Cataloging-in-Publication Data
Balbo, Ned, 1959–
    Lives of the sleepers / Ned Balbo.
        p.   cm. — (The Ernest Sandeen prize in poetry ; 2005)
    ISBN 0-268-02184-8 (acid-free paper)
    ISBN 0-268-02185-6 (pbk. : acid-free paper)
    I. Title.   II. Series.
    PS3552.A4454L58   2005
    811'.54—dc22
                                                            2005001229

∞ *This book is printed on acid-free paper.*

Contents

I I I

Acknowledgments

Thanks are due to the editors of publications in which some of these poems first appeared or are forthcoming:

> *Antioch Review:* "Cycles of Catastrophe in Petrarch"
> *Crab Orchard Review:* "First Thaw"; "Ophelia: A Wreath"
> *Dogwood:* "Lives of the Sleepers"; "Two Departures"
> *Ekphrasis:* "Dante's Beatrice"
> *Interim:* "Eurydice in Darkness"
> *Italian Americana:* "Scapular"; "A Stranger's Arms"; "Orpheus and His Muse"
> *Möbius:* "Novena"
> *River Styx:* "Expectation of a Journey"
> *Schuylkill Valley Journal:* "Second Circle"; "Widow"; "Desire: A Bestiary: [Magnificent Frigate-Bird]; [Banana Slug]; [Bonobo]"

"After Hitchcock," "Pomegranate," "Millennial," and "House of Song" first appeared in *Notre Dame Review.*

"Aristaeus Forgiven" received the 2003 Robert Frost Foundation Poetry Award.

I want to extend special gratitude to Alfred Corn, William Gifford, Dana Gioia, Judith Hall, Andrew Hudgins, Charles Martin, John Matthias, David St. John, Jane Satterfield, and Elizabeth Spires for their encouragement or editorial suggestions. Thanks also to the Robert Frost Foundation, the Loyola College Center for the Humanities, the Sewanee Writers' Conference, the Virginia Center for the Creative Arts, and the West Chester University Poetry Conference for welcome support.

"Eroded Cupid" is for Liz Albert.

LIVES OF THE
SLEEPERS

I

The stiff Heart questions was it He, that bore,
And Yesterday, or Centuries before?

— Emily Dickinson

In my dreams the world dies also in white embers

— David St. John

Desire: A Bestiary

Magnificent Frigate-Bird

Where is your nesting site?
Mud-spattered branch, or tree—
even the ground will do.
Time, now, to raise your voice,
your skilled falsetto, skyward
as if to summon down
from extraordinary flight
a mate, her wings spread wide—
Your throat-sac quivers, bright balloon
from which song bursts
too late, too soon,
your head near-swallowed
by the pulsing of your throat.

Peacock

A child, in summer, I'd wake up to screams,
Great squalls cut short, but cannot say how long
It took—how many summers—till I felt
One day, I had to find their source: beyond
Slashed nets of wire, two large birds circling
Each other, slowly, in a stranger's yard.
One shrieked, so close this time that I jumped back,
Startled as bright eyes stammered in a fan
That spread, outward and upward—blue, green, gold,
And bronze metallic flashings—folding back
Into itself when he had made his point
After a dozen circles, tail-coverts
Dragged, now, through the dust. The peahen watched,
Called back, not yet impressed. I watched as well,

Waiting for what would happen when the shrieks
Boiled up again, feeling a neighbor's glare
Upon me as I trespassed. And when they did,
What I remember best are gusts of color
Hurled through dust, raised quills, a light that touched
Glazed feathers into motion or collapse
As I stood still and listened—
                                                    There it is,
Again, her voice nothing at all like yours,
Bright music that I still hear; there it is,
Once more, this dull hen's plumage nothing like
Your gold hair in the dusk, fanned out against
The dark bed where you sleep; and here I am,
No cry but these few words meant to preserve
What still is precious in what time remains.

A Stranger's Arms

Cupid and Psyche

"If he who keeps you in this splendid palace
Were a man, would he remain concealed
Always in darkness, following kind words
With warnings, gifts with threats?" The charge cut deeply,
Sisters urging doubt. But when the lamp
Drew light across the stone floor, tapestries
Inlaid with gold, to show him—man and god,
The night's lovemaking over—sound asleep
Back in his bed, quite still, she stood there, stunned:
So this was he who kept himself in shadow,
Waking as hot oil spilled. . . .
                              As for us,
Locked close this one last night in total darkness,
All we once knew in bright light disappears
Into fierce kisses, flesh, a stranger's arms.

After Hitchcock

1. *Descent and Aftermath*

A long fall toward the grave, then toward the roof
Below the bell-tower, freefall into flight
That ends on impact—yours. Or hers. Or both.
And afterward, bowed strings filling the air,
Black disk spinning in place, you sit and stare
Expressionless: cramped room, and one old friend
Who won't let go, however far you fall,
No words to tell her if you're spinning still
In blackness or in light. How long she waits
We don't know, but no one should wait that long,
And when she turns, each slow step down the hall
Seems endless, like the space that swallows her,
Bottomless corridor . . . *Pointless to stay,*
She knows by now. *This patient needs his rest.*

2. *Madeleine's Afterlife*

Those weeks after the bell-tower—safe, alone,
A rented room, the green light of the sign
Hotel Empire left burning every night—
I felt, at last, I'd freed myself from her,
Suits pushed back in the closet, jewels set down
And shut away. Once only, hands half-healed
(Sharp twine and paper cuts) I left the store,
Just one more working girl "wandering" home
(That loaded word) on foot, and thought, *How good
It would be now to slip into her life
A few more hours: to drive, sealed off from noise,
Crude pickups, and the rest, gliding down streets
Silent and dizzying . . .* How good to fall,
Weightless, toward water, knowing that you saw.

3. *Melanie's Ascent as Metaphor*

Their explanations always seem absurd:
Thick men (except for Ingrid) filling suits
That look inflammable, who drone on, glazed
Eyes fixed on some far point beyond the storm
Of their own rhetoric. We turn away
When Hitchcock asks and answers once again
What's madness? through the words of one who *knows*,
Some tensed psychiatrist . . . And yet, transfixed,
We watch as Melanie, flashlight in hand,
Begins her slow ascent late in a film
Where madness goes unmentioned, as she stops
Before the door she fears, then steps inside,
Glance frozen upward: shattered roof, blue sky—
Exploding from the bed, a thousand wings.

Desire: A Bestiary

Honey Bee

Surrounded and caressed, honey
presented for her feast,
a queen will rest, stiff hairs groomed

by her retinue of drones
who close in through the hum
gently, a swarm of many wings—

But come the sudden impulse,
what is kindness? Nothing else:
hive forsaken, fast in flight, she'll seek

new company, lovers dispersed
over a greater realm,
hovering through consummations

accomplished in mid-air . . .
                              But one
moment spent too near
costs each his life when she tears out

what made him dear.

Lives of the Saints

Saints Agnes, Catherine of Siena, Tiresias, Rita, Lucy,
Lawrence, Barbara, Dymphna, Elizabeth of Hungary

Bow down . . . So easy to obey, so much
The same as what He asks. But when you rise
Your hands slip from the chains, a child's hands,
Still frail and small, too small. The guardsman laughs,
Ties back your wrists, and all begins again:
"I am *His* bride," you cry, your clothes stripped off
To laughter, howls, wolf-whistles, and sheeps' bones
Hurled from the crowd; but when the mob pulls back—
Some poor soul struck by lightning—you've used up
Those miracles, those lucky accidents,
That saw you through till now, the sword raised high—
Bow down, don't think of it. All ties renounced,
What will remain, finally, but these small lives
Given to us: great faith, great anguish, bliss

Past any mortal love, while casualties
Mount up? These are the candidates for sainthood.
Those who defy their parents and will not marry;
Those who put on dark robes and beat their breast,
Crying aloud; who rake their own flesh, praying
Softly for comfort; those who are held in flames,
Untouched by fire; those bound to the stake, who burn;
Those who emerge unscathed. . . . A soul in grace,
Shining, may hover in pale light, past thick smoke
Still rising from ashes: a vision to comfort those
Who suffer but, reassured, can die at peace.
Or, like the boy-protector of the host,
Those who discover a purpose and a grace
Sacred enough to die for: clubbed with sticks,

Pummelled with rocks, forced down until he bled,
Yet thankful as well for this great clarity
Granted to one so young. Or those grown old,
Kept from the world: a widow whose husband beat her,

Bowed to the Cross, might pray for one great Passion,
One last Pain like the light which, swelling, blinds her,
Rising before her eyes as one thorn falls,
Strikes home—or so she'll insist to those who mop
The blood from her brow and marvel at the wound.
Wounds sometimes heal; sometimes they reappear,
As on the palms, torn hands raised to the light,
Transforming day by day: flesh fills the seams,
Skin peels, and blends; even the scars are gone.
And yet, beyond stigmata, there are wounds

We might call self-inflicted: wounds they *seek*,
Life-threatening, and welcome. Think of one
Whose governor had vowed to see her fall,
Turning her clear gaze upward to declare,
"You're wrong. I'll never sin. My heart is pure,
A temple of the Spirit"—one who speaks
Her own mind with such purity of vision,
And such will, she's bound to feel let down
When all her prayers are answered but the pain
Falls short, somehow, despite that pure heart pierced,
One thrust from a soldier's sword, her own bright blood
Flooding the ground. Only the holy bread
Touched to her tongue transports her. Think of one
Who spoke his wish to die—whose Pope remarked,

"You will," as captors took him—who, still roasting
On the gridiron, dares to shout, "It's time
To turn me over; that side's done": both *sought*
Their fates; both recognized and seized, at last,
One moment when they'd most become *themselves*.
Others have faced the choice between two fathers—
He who made us, He who made the world—
As in the case of one who woke alone,
Bleeding and bruised, who rose in tears to ask
One Father for mercy—not for herself, but for
The weaker, mortal sire: and when she saw
That dazed man on the ledge, finally defeated
By his daughter's will, compelled to take
This final step his greater will required,

Did she, too, bow her head? And in the fire
That streamed from the skies, consuming him, what did
This mere man make of her expression—calm,
Cut off in mid-prayer for his heartlessness—
Frozen a few yards distant from her body?
(A common fate, for saints.) Once, when a chief
Of great wealth lost his wife, undone by grief,
He sought her lookalike all over Ireland,
Sending his men on quests he must have known
Were doomed to fail, waiting while each vain effort
Narrowed his options till one course alone
Remained: the path long planned: to call his daughter
To his chamber, gently stroke her hair
Shadowed in candlelight; to touch her shoulder,

And astonish her with the proposal
She could not accept. . . . And so it goes:
Starving themselves, flesh torn, heads struck from bodies,
Plunged into fire, old wounds resurfacing,
Always a pure gaze trained on sun and sky—
These are the lives we seek: lives of the saints.
And yet, of all these, I will think of you
Most often, Princess, bearing beneath your cloak
Bread for the poor, trudging the mountain path
Through dust and rockfall on your long descent
From castle, servant, sun. Not far below,
Your Prince awaits you still, resolved to ask
Some small sign of regard, parting your robe—
Here, where the petals press against your skin.

Blessing

By use of the formula "Even now" . . .
the lover recreates their love at the same
time that he regrets their separation . . .
  —Barbara Stoler Miller, introduction to
    her translation of Bilhana's *Love-Thief*

I miss her body even now,
Her hair in disarray, pale flowers
That tangle as they fall, a face
Not yet shadowed by loss, no grace

Beyond her as I watch. But will
She hear me if short syllables
Are spoken slowly, if these words
Last long, the sharp point of a sword

Drawn slowly in and out? What wound
Afflicts her, trembling girl, whose hand
Searches against me as I move
Closer, to kiss her neck, who proves

Tireless at dawn, in any light?
I miss her even now—by night
Struck bells and peacock-shrieks, by day
Gull-cries and gold hair clinging . . . May

She still be laughing while she parts
Lank wet hair in the mirror, shirt
Unbuttoned as she stands, skin wet
Where still a few drops trail—what petals

Touch her bare back, or her bed?
Tonight, of all she hears or reads,
May these words bring most blessing: jewelled
Lamps polished, set aflame, reveal—

As long as words can speak—pearls soft,
Haloed, resistant as they lift,
Tongue-touched or pressed; pink bitten lips
Now bruised, wine-smeared; this "perfect cup"

I gently search—yes, even now,
Bilhana would approve—for slow
Fast "rising falling rhythms," moments
Crossing toward a present tense

Which threatens not to end, but does . . .
If words arise from shadows, loss
Made sharper with each breath, the space
Between us going dark, whose face

Do I remember even now?
Shiva does not avoid the fire
That boils up from the ocean's floor,
Bright lava-poisoned depths; somehow,

A shriveled tortoise bears the earth
Upon his shell and, faithful, keeps
His promises before he sleeps—
All moments of surpassing worth.

Antique Ring

Lately the seed-pearls in this antique ring
Keep falling out. (From odd Victoriana
Sifted carefully, small gleaming thing
You treasured once, our *lux perpetua*:
Pure, untarnished gold. Fallen from favor.)
Back to the dealer—old maid, all alone:
"Who was the original engraver?"
So much fine, frail etching . . . Two pearls gone,
One more to go, this time, and then, once more,
The same sad cycle of small gains, large losses
Overpowering us. Walk round the store.
She looks for seed-pearls, small tears, guesses
This time it'll last? Look how it ended,
And began. Full circle. Empty-handed.

Psyche

What holds me here? Carved walls, a vaulted roof,
Harp-strings and lyre struck invisibly,
All wealth I can imagine, tapestry
Of shepherdess and flock, all day the light
From windows out of reach. He'll come tonight
And leave by morning, unseen, not enough
To touch this bruise, beard-scratches, fading mark
Across red skin, abandoned . . . In the dark
He'll ask, *What else remains? You've all you need*
Right here: pillars of gold, desire made flesh,
All that you ask for, given. Well, not *all,*
A shadow fallen on silk robes, one wish
Denied: to glimpse him, only once. But will
I want to stay, that one wish satisfied?

Fever

I gave myself to him because I thought
It wouldn't—couldn't—last. Could I be wrong?
But when I woke months later into white
Space filling up the room, sound without meaning
Pushing itself inside (all that noise,
Blows struck, blank noise of traffic) I felt—gone,
Erased, part of his world: laughter of boys
Passing outside, this bed, another sun
Forced through the curtains: Gone, and him asleep,
After so many sleepless hours at sea,
This blackness, dizzying. . . . If I could keep
The whole world calm, each branch still, and an eye
On shapes rising from shadow, I could feel,
Finally, that I myself could rise, at will,

To feel the world slip out of my control,
Then back again, never too fast or far
Yet far enough to wake within each cell,
Charged nerve, and muscle white light like this fire
That scorches earth again. And just as well.
What am I waiting for? More sunlight, power
To stay or go? Stained plaster ceiling, kill
Or be killed? Shadows flexing on the floor—
Two animals, like us, who rise and fall
Then cry at last, in one voice, nothing more
Than two souls falling from what's visible
To what will never be—Cry out, the shore
Recedes still further, hold on, or lie still,
Reach out, or run away—all we can bear—

Grief, love, and pain—is ours. . . . But this must end.
Think of it: souls in fusion, while smeared dishes
Clatter in some sink; to feel his hand
Press down, my hair pulled, fingers tensed, what flashes

Pomegranate

Persephone in Hades

Not free will but
narcissus brought
you here, cold realm
beyond the world,
where caverns hold
so much, a dead
sea beautiful
in darkness: tri-
lobite engraved
in rock, shells fused
to cave-walls split
and fissured, swirls
of strata, corpse's
hair. Don't be

afraid. Look at
these creatures: fish
long skeletal,
etched overhead,
preserved—how long
before they, too,
had changed,
drawn to
these depths? Such art
is forged in sol-
itude. It is
what lasts: mortal
remains, or else
mere imprints left

to chance, fragments
discarded, fos-
silized. A world
apart. Even

16

Now, in him? In me? To keep in rhythm
And to lose ourselves, to rise, look down
And see him lie back, stunned; to look at him
And wonder, When? What next? *To know the sun*
Now rising must crash down, to glimpse the moon,
Sliced through and scissor-like, already close
To vanishing once more . . . Will it be soon?
To choke back fear and grief; to feel this loss
Like others—all of them—hover as if
To strike the instant we feel safe enough

To give ourselves over at last. . . . And when it's over
(Wet mouth wiped on belly, sheets pulled taut,
Ourselves again, sinking as if in fever)
Is any music left? No matter what
He says, it's over, was when it began,
Will be if it goes on. . . . Once, I heard rain
Striking the window, slowly, this one man
Falling away . . . If we could look again,
Tracing the accidents that brought us here,
And then deserted us, what would we find
On lost streets, in lost rooms, or anywhere?
More accidents—our lives—built in a wind
That lashes harder till they break apart—
That lashes out until we break, the hurt

Greater as we resist . . . I can't go on.
This whirl of hair and hips, wrists clutched, skin caught,
And pressed, raked, bit, and smoothed, quick thrusts to skin
Or flesh, resistance—slowly now—white light
Filling the room, the deep white space within
Us both—how can it be sustained? All night,
All morning, all our lives? That morning when
Light poured in, blinding us, I saw the threat,
Fought off the thought, got up and acted then
As if nothing had happened, and I bought
It, too, or thought I did: that this won't wane,
Or fade, or die soon; that the very thought
Of touching him that first time could be born
Without the shadow that would black it out.

those flowers, cupped
coronas bent
toward sun,
broke free
from layers of earth,
ice-bound, and don't
forget they drew
you downward. . . . If
you'd stay here will-
ingly, forced light

of equinox
renounced, perhaps
your mother's grief
would lift. Give me
your palm, pale skin
I love. And if
you still decide
to flee, accept
this small gift, broken
fruit, flawed heart
forced open by
my thumb, sticky
with juice, wet
chambered

flesh, tissue
torn free of rind
and calyx, pulp
expendable
at best, and let
it drop into
the dark. Forget
the voices, all
their murmuring,
what strikes but fails
to sting, and feel
upon your tongue
only the smooth,
shelled seed.

Second Circle

The Inferno, Canto V, Robert Pinsky's version

Hell in perpetual motion: hurricane
That twists us upward and apart, great wind
Unending, force that bears us, rends us limb
From aching limb, great storm, won't you slow down?
Won't you pause for one moment, let us fall
Once more against those rocks, however sharp
Below us, there to rest and catch our breath
As, in life, we did not? So many souls,
Such bodies passing over, couplings
Never to be re-lived, or never known,
So many who died strangers, more lost souls
Thrown past each other, pummelled for all time
By winds and cross-winds, calling out, alone,
To all those we would gladly touch again.

Desire: A Bestiary

Damselfly

Paternity-obsessed,
the damselfly divests
his partner of some other's seed.
Stick-like, silver-blue,
he glides behind her,
taps her with an organ
formed for this one purpose:
to scoop away the cells
deposited by rivals.
Caught up and stuck fast,
he's instinctively aware
while quivering on a reed
for a moment, or an hour,
she's known this act before.
Jealous escort, anxious follower,
let go—
        And when she drops,
against the water's surface,
take care to clasp her firmly,
clustered eggs set for release
and take no thought of any
who will follow.

Millennial

Across Minnesota, in Wisconsin and South Dakota,
and as far away as Quebec and Vermont, scientists
and residents are seeing frogs with grotesquely
misshapen limbs and tails, missing or shrunken eyes,
and smaller than normal sex-organs. . . . Scientists
are not sure what is causing the deformities.
                    — *The New York Times*, October 13, 1996

How did it start? A thinning of the ozone,
Ultraviolet glare, a fish-net's swish
Through pond scum, and epiphany: *These frogs*
Are monsters, tangled helplessly, their limbs
Too many or too few. Or else not frogs
But some new threat, a curse, unwanted foundlings
Stunned beneath the sun, their bodies' change

Triggered by microscopic parasites,
That cue the flesh: *form legs*, failed limbs that flop
Out of unlikely places, blight observed
Under "ideal" conditions, in the lab.
Afflicted frogs. Small monsters. *Pour the vials*
Of God's wrath on the earth, as unclean spirits
Leap from the dragon's mouth, the beast's, the prophet's,

Masters of false miracles. "When frogs,
All four limbs missing, started turning up,
I knew we had a problem"—*all* of us,
Not just the luckless, dazed amphibian
Wriggling in tepid water, or the next,
A few legs dangling, clustered at the hip,
One good leg kicking hard. A sentinel species,

Leopard frogs suffer the world's effects
Sooner than we (by decades? Centuries?
No way to tell). The warning signs converge—
How did it start? A frog's ontogeny

(Gelled egg through tadpole), secretly revised,
Hurls forward, evolution misdirected,
Garbled by what agent? "Something in

The water," speculation goes—synthetic
Retinoids, perhaps, that trick the body,
Cells misfiring, plague of altered frogs
Infesting mud and marsh. What will deceive
Our bodies—force or substance, accident,
Genetic postscript—leaving us transformed,
Lines of descent disrupted, broken off?

We're foundering already, sperm counts fallen,
Cells in steep decline, conceptions flawed—
The river shall bring forth frogs, abundantly,
To crawl into your house, inside your chamber,
And upon your bed—a waning flood
Lost in suspension, swelled heads stuffed with strands
Of useless DNA. Look past the flesh

Toward grief that drains the spirit, and beyond—
To X-rays, penicillin, leaded fumes
Engulfing traffic, pesticides released,
Sprayed over farms, mixed into feed, with flesh
Turned butchered meat—are these the cause? Consider
Methoprene, which purges swamp and wetlands
Of all but itself, insecticide

Dissolved when sunlight, pond, and protozoa
Break it down to pseudo-retinoids
That bring about still more monstrosities—
Or maybe not. An endless stream of theories,
Half-truths unresolved. How *did* it start,
But more: how will it end? What factors bend
Frogs into strange shapes, blind them, kill off sperm

Cells, fan through water, iridescent arc,
Or unseen poison, source invisible?
I think of Hope—the infant, not our own
Willed blindness toward conclusion—born a rare

Twin, sister undeveloped, yet conjoined,
Immersed in flesh, form swimming from a body,
Half emerged, arm reaching through the darkness

Of another's skin, a second spine
That breaks the surface, third leg wrongly placed,
Fourth hand affixed to hip: four surgeries,
Two months since birth, unwilling egg that never
Fully split, still clinging, cut away
In cautious stages, to reveal, at last,
One child left whole. . . . How did it start? A thousand

Years from now, we'll know. Or someone will.
And all with neither fins nor scales, nor all
That leap in rivers, flailing, shall you eat—
These are abominations. So we cut
Away the defects, hope that what remains
Survives the effort: faint thrum, throat-sacs swelled
With steady croaking, calls to mate, a noise

Returned as song, pond trembling at the touch
Of sound limbs, swift recoil. Or song reduced
To silence, revelation come to all—
Foreknowledge proven, prophecy fulfilled,
Vision confirmed, lives vanished? Nothing sure
Except, despite the dark, this certainty:
Eyes not ours will behold a world transformed.

In Avignon

Petrarch sees "Laura" for the first time, April 6, 1327

In Avignon, the monstrance of St. Clare
In place above the altar, eucharist
Set high for all to see, worshippers blessed
Beneath transfigured flesh, I touched your hair,
Or would have, if I'd dared to come so near,
Ring scarcely visible. The moment passed,
But as the crowd swarmed through the doors, the best
Of what was left to me—more penance, prayer,
And poetry—rose up before my eyes,
One flash of light: one moment. When I see
You always at a distance, all the lies
I'll tell myself from now on, secretly,
Will fuse to one: transfigured flesh, a maze
Of passages, all dark, encircling me.

A Tragedy

A tragedy of Shakespearean proportions
Scaled down for the suburbs and a cast
Of gifted amateurs: two "honors" kids,
Lovesick eighth-graders not long disappeared
For whom the worst was feared, and now is over,
Dragged up from the river, final words
Slipped under rocks impossible to miss:
My mother tried to break us up forever—
Her mother!—*Now we're going to a place
Where, at last, we'll always be together . . .*
You poor kids. Snapshots fade, the news moves on,
And though we dread the solace that you sought
And found, still more we fear not to have loved
As deeply, nor as recklessly, as you.

Fire Victim

Once, boarding the train to New York City,
The aisle crowded and all seats filled, I glimpsed
An open space—more pushing, stuck in place—
And then saw why: a man, face peeled away,
Sewn back in haste, skin grafts that smeared like wax
Spattered and frozen, one eye flesh-filled, smooth,
One cold eye toward the window. Cramped, shoved hard,
I, too, passed up the seat, the place, and fought on
Through to the next car, and the next, but now
I wonder why the fire that could have killed him
Spared him, burns scarred over; if a *life*
Is what he calls this space through which he moves,
Dark space we dared not enter, and what fire
Burns in him when he sees us move away.

II

It becomes still more difficult to find
Words at once true and kind,
Or not untrue and not unkind.

— Philip Larkin

If you don't come flying into the future,
where will I meet you? . . .

— Marilyn Hacker

Avalokitesvara

O Lord who never turns from suffering,
Celestial Bodhisattva, archetype
Of all compassion, you who emanate
A million more Enlightened Ones, all selfless,
All yourself, a thousand saving hands
Prepared to ease our passage, guardian
In this life and the next, and in between,
I want to live as you did, eons past,
Before ten pairs of eyes beheld our pain,
Hands clasped in prayer still grasping, all you'd need—
The Three Jewels—still beyond your reach, strange days
When you had but one body and one heart,
Blood-flower opening slowly, breaking free
Of all attachment . . . Shining, deity.

Entries in the Dream Book

"A"

To travel *abroad*, in dreams—this is desire
To fly far from our own lives, even if
To do so risks an *accident at sea*—
What we fear most but, waking, won't admit:
Abandonment: the dread of swirling fast
Among the lost; resigned, we sink from view
And, later, look up "drowning" under "D."
The book includes them all: each metaphor—
Excuse me, "symbol"—entered and explained
For lovers like ourselves, *anxious* for signs,
Some knowledge that gives guidance—anything
That offers certainty of joy or sorrow—
Either will do these weeks that the *abyss*
Below goes dark, grows wide, and threatens us.

"M"

. . . Till out of darkness trails a *melody*,
Omen of friendship—old friends if the tune
Is long-familiar, new ones if the tune
Is one we've never heard. What if a man
Pours *milk* upon a woman? He desires her
And, in dreams at least, fulfills his wish—
Symbolically, that is. And hers as well.
And yet, the same dream may reveal, repressed,
A yearning for *Mother*'s breast . . . And when
The *music* streaming through our dreams threatens
To run forever, every thought a cry
To absent friends, or lovers far away,
Who'll choose to listen this time? Then, who'll turn
Her back again? Who'll cradle us once more?

"N"

This *necklace* is for you this *night* (black space,
Charged negative of day) when every pearl
Of wet light clings to moss, when lovers meet
As if drawn to this threshold between night
And all we know, or will admit to knowing.
Nothing matters, nothing holds us back,
Or does it? We're held fast, the Dream Book says,
Because true lovers recognize desire
Last of all, though all the world looks on.
If it were possible to meet again
As once we did so easily, we'd see
The promise that surrounds us: not dead space
Where all we build, frail *nests* that cannot last,
Is washed away unseen, and nothing rests.

"D"

Don't be afraid to dream about *despair:*
Beyond the *desert* lies a lush oasis
Soon to be found, as we ourselves will be,
Among palms and clear water, gusts of wind
That blow the *dust* away—dust-grains, like *diamonds*
Glittering, then *disappearing* fast,
The silence filling us and all the air
Around us as we call, just damaged goods
"Discarded"? There's no entry for the word.
Diamonds, despair, and dust. We disappear.
And yet, to dream of diamonds also means
That fortune finds us out, wherever we hide,
If we survive what wounds us deeply and
Can keep a safer distance from despair.

Abandonment. Reunion. Melody.

Abandonment, reunion; melody,
Or silence; night and day; daybreak, then dusk,
And back again, the language we select
Implies its opposite: wet clay, dry sand,
Or falling water stilled: we scan our dreams
For signs, and find them: *angels* that are changed
To *arrows* as we watch, connection sought
And always found, connection in itself
What we most seek, *masks* off and mercy shown;
And if, our *names* erased, we *dream* at last
Of one word only, let it be a sound
That shines like *amethyst*, that shakes the dust
From these dead pages, that restores what's lost
When all we've seen returns as Metaphor.

Two in Discord

1. *Orpheus and His Muse*
   After Edmond Aman Jean's painting

This I take to be Thrace: the "wild solitudes"
In which you wandered, lyre in hand, past huts
And haystacks, through tall grass, late summer sky
Surging above you, bound by memory
Of one you couldn't abandon but still failed,
Somehow, on brink of daylight. So you walk,
One day like all the rest—weeds, chicory,
Wildflowers and grass-blades, bloodroot—all alone
But for this Muse, white-winged, who walks beside
You, shadowed face a blur, hand on your heart,
Who steadies you when you weaken, hair touched red
This hour of the day's dying, the blue-gold sky
Streaming away still faster, and you play
On ceaselessly, play as you've always done.

2. *Eurydice in Darkness*

I didn't think that you'd descend so soon
Into this world beneath the world, these caves
Of ice, cold light of asphodel, this dress
Itself a pale light floating over waters
As I pass: first, Fire; Forgetfulness;
Then fallen shadows. In such light, devotion
Seems too pure, too blinded in its power
Not to destroy us both. And yet, such faith
Has brought you here. . . . The song completes itself.
I follow, head bowed, as if I believe
That we'll transcend this darkness if we climb
Faster and far enough, that all your words,
Melodious sounds, can save us? If you turn,
You'll see me as I am: already lost.

Widow

What is *widow?* Weeds. Black veil and dress.
Smudged eye-shadow, dark nights. Smell of his shirt
Still crumpled in the closet. Emptiness.
Caged bird at sun-up, crying. At the heart
Of every light, more pain. *Widow* is calls
From old friends, those who've heard, who haven't heard,
Measuring every silence. Rain that falls
From gutters onto dirt, singing this word
You've heard and laughed off, found was one you knew,
Then spoke yourself: *widow.* A photograph
Washed out. Failures of memory, what's true,
What isn't, blurred together. Long enough
By now? *Never.* A grief that casts its shadow,
Fallen, on wet leaves . . . Inhuman. *Widow.*

Cast Away, Recovered

1. Eroded Cupid

An old friend found him on a beach in Greece
"Where gypsies camp," she laughs: eroded Cupid,
Three limbs broken off, features rubbed out
By time and tide—what else?—gold wing-tips chipped,
Nose severed, gaze intact. The perfect gift,
She knows: something once beautiful, now broken,
Grinning vacantly as if to bless
Deluded lovers, lives at risk, together
For the moment, souls swept out to sea,
Drowned, or about to be. . . .
                            Her mother walked
That beach, a Greek's new widow, daughter watching
From the rocks. Stepfather newly dead,
She glanced down at the sand: just more debris
To salvage, leave, or throw back to the sea.

2. Scorpion Conch

Seven notched stalks: one points directly south,
The top one north, the rest a flattened hand
Of tensed arthritic fingers. Shades of brown,
Or orange, splashed with white across a surface
Knobbed and gnarled: this mollusk's carapace
Brittle, ceramic almost, shield and armor
Borne in every weather, now abandoned
To the elements. Safe to turn over

For a different view: bright gleam that slides
On polished skin beneath our gaze, a lip
Flushed peach; of course this crevice: long smooth arc
That slices upward—shadowed, purple-ridged—
Right here, where damp flesh, salt-smell of the ocean
Once clung fast and, touched, was drawn back in.

Desire: A Bestiary

Deep-Sea Angler Fish

You dwell at enormous depths,
body translucent, luminous,
dangling the photophore
that illuminates and lures,
never alone, escorts trailing,
their tiny jaws locked shut
in marvelous symbiosis!
Courtship and marriage fused—
Last rites, too?
                    —for over time, your own skin
spreads into a shroud
that draws them in, blind suitors
turned appendages, mere organs
that deliver seed, bodies
lost, fully, to you—

But as they forget themselves,
do you forget them, too:
souls clinging near enough
to call forth
in your need.

The Kiss in Shadow

The kiss in shadow . . . Arc of your neck, dark cleft,
& lasting grief . . . Fast ripening past decay,
Squeezed hard. Nothing but rotten pulp, all seed
& pale, clumped flesh. A waste: your voice gone cold,
Crying from far off now . . . Sharp thrusts, an aching
Glorious while it lasted, days and nights—
How did we lose them all? What takes their place
In these dark months . . . Or did we lose our bliss
Because bright hues look faded without contrast
To darker shades, darkness . . . So much fades fast
In memory, now, though surging near the surface,
Sometimes, there's the glimmer of lost flesh,
Sleek silver fur, slicked down . . . It vanishes,
Always . . . Dark cleft, breast-arc. Face in shadow . . .

Crucible

At last I understand: what seemed at first
Mere pain wrought without thought was meant to burn
Away the surface-flesh, peel back the weak,
Stringed muscle and thin skin till what was left
Was strong enough to last, stretched taut and aching
With this death, this birth, this stripped-away
Still-throbbing break with all that went before—
And, more: to prove that this, too, could be pleasure—
Scorched skin, love withheld, the pointed promise
Of renewal offered at some cost—
Bare need exposed to ridicule—till, finally,
Raw wounds pressed, raised to the light once more
To burn or heal ourselves, we burn again—
For us to find our pleasure in that burning.

House of Wax

After Andre de Toth's 1953 remake
of Michael Curtiz's 1933 film
Mystery of the Wax Museum

I knew you instantly. Chained to the stake,
Stacked kindling underfoot, your eyes locked on
Some far-off radiance beyond the cross
Raised skyward on its staff: Saint Joan of Arc
Marked by your clothes, black hair, an icon's gaze,
Completely motionless, the gaslamps bright
Against the walls surrounding fresh tableaux
Of history and horror—Anne Boleyn
Brought to the headsman's block; Lincoln's assassin
Caught in the act, offstage; Charlotte Corday,
Knife drawn before Marat steeped in his bath,
Perpetually surprised—creatures of wax,
Except for you, Cathy? I knew the sculptor,
Henry Jarrod, poor soul, had been burned,
Hands ruined by the fire that swept his first
Great gallery. Near crippled, he'd survived,
Somehow, to stage this comeback, all he'd lost
Rebuilt at last, a life's work charred to wreckage
Now restored. But how? I stood alone,
Still breathing your perfume. *I must be wrong,*
I thought, and yet stepped forward, found my footing
On the firewood, reached out, grieving monk
In sackcloth crouched nearby in tears of mourning
As I touched your flesh, withdrew, climbed down,
And hid my face. *It couldn't be. It was—*
Dead ringer in wax, pale sculpture of a saint
Resigned that burning was the price for bliss,
Or Cathy Gray, my roommate, murdered friend
Snatched from the morgue, her body never found?
Till now. I turned away, twin braziers crackling
Near the Nile-banks, close to Cleopatra

39

Basking near the blaze with Antony.
Elsewhere, a crowd drew back, blurted its praise
For each new figure stationed on the brink
Of some defining act: "This modern Bluebeard
Killed not wisely but too well," the artist's
Irony lost on schoolgirls gazing up
Bleakly, in awe, nudged forward to the next
Doomed love or crime of passion as the tour
Fled past in fear, delight.
                              I found myself
Rejoined by Scott, himself a struggling sculptor,
Escort and old friend: "Sue, are you crying?"
Couldn't he see? I told him, though he smiled,
Wearied, "It's wax, my dear!" Nothing amiss,
No crime concealed in plain sight, nothing wrong
Except myself, of course, who'd found you strangled,
Now just "seeing things."
                              "You're right, my dear—
It's more than a chance resemblance," the master sculptor,
Hearing me, broke in. So this was Jarrod,
Tour complete, voice steady, wheelchair-bound,
Voice gentler as he glanced up with a smile
—*No matter that I'd glimpsed one ear's faint piercing
Through the wax?* I wanted to believe,
As he claimed, that the *Herald*'s grainy photos
In reports after your vanishing
Had fascinated him so much he'd shaped
St. Joan to look like you. Graying, goateed,
He spoke with elegance, gloved hands quite still,
To ask, finally, in reasonable tones,
Would you have minded? "No . . . " It was my turn
To offer reassurance, though I heard,
Instead, your voice that night, laced boots and corset
Pulled taut as we'd laughed, the landlady
In fury at our noise—last mirror-check,
Red hat perfectly balanced for your date—
"Distinguished looking, older than I like them"—
Cooling his heels downstairs. What could I say?
I'd wished you luck, and should have wished you more,
Wronged murder victim, now a martyred saint

Who loomed above us, every detail caught
And verified, as Scott would boast once Jarrod
Hired him on, apprentice to an art
Beyond the master's seared, unsteady hands.
The day's grand opening a great success,
Scott reached out; Jarrod shook his hand, squeezing
It tightly. *How small all of us must seem
To him*, I felt, who spends his days compelled
To plunder history, arrange and freeze
Its dark, heart-wrenching scenes, who seeks the dead—
Saints, assassins, lovers, murderers—
In crowds, the world's blurred photos, figures raised
To unimagined heights, the artist reaching
Through your neck to fix each eye within
Its socket, slowly; later still, to seal
Your head in its proper place, plaster-of-Paris
Body framed by metal, sprayed and smoothed
With cauldron-boiled wax.
                              But I was right,
I found, when I returned to the museum
One last time, the only living person
After hours among the reenactments,
Haunted still, on impulse peeling back
The black wig, braided human hair, to find
The bright gold underneath—*your* hair, Cathy,
Your body on exhibit. "All I'd loved
Was taken from me," said Jarrod as if this
Were all the explanation I would need.
He rose from shadow, standing as I always
Should have known he could, convinced that words
Could justify the risks he took for art,
Fierce eyes trained on my face, searching for likeness
Others would have missed, Scott sent off blindly
On some needless errand. So I stood
Trembling with rage: *Who'll send the spark this time,
Ignite the blaze till Jarrod and his "people"
Burn up where they stand, creator plunging
Through the fire, enraged, a gas-line hissing,
Fueling the inferno, Booth in flames,*

Another artist-criminal's skin melting
In the heat, face smoothed to caricature,
England's monarch beheaded as his neck—
Warm, softened plaster—wilts, the dead unveiled,
Displayed, near skeletal: some huge explosion
Strong enough to wipe them off the earth—
A crematorium. Where could I go?
I fought him off, swung wildly, struck his face
But felt—not flesh: the mask broke, brittle wax
Falling away in pieces to reveal
Monster, predator—the gentleman
You'd thought distinguished, Cathy, his disguise
Shattered for good. . . .
                              But then, as I blacked out
In Jarrod's hold, certain I'd share your fate,
The face I thought more monstrous was the other's,
Long familiar, one who'd find, appalled,
When he returned, that he'd misplaced his trust,
Calling in vain, who'd point detectives toward
The chamber where his mentor, feverish,
Fused Art and Life—the fatal crucible
Close to the boiling point, the artist's vision
Nearly fulfilled; one who'd say, if asked,
He'd taken part in no crime, conscience eased
To think he'd rescued me, a face controlled,
Not burned beyond repentance or repair
But always loyal. Blank gaze. Frozen smile.

Queenright

A thriving hive is "queenright." But not
any queen will do. Problems in a hive
are often traced back to the queen and,
still further, to the errors of the beekeeper.

Perhaps in haste you caught and killed your queen
Then acted slowly while the colony
Moved fast to fill her place. Or, having split
The hive, one queen for a diminished realm,
None for the rest, you brought to those abandoned
One they drove off, forced down, or devoured.
Many mistakes are possible. Think hard.
Perhaps your queen is missing, lost in flight,
Murdered before she mated, fallen ill
Without your knowledge, while some lookalike
Successor rules the court. Or else you sought
Unwisely—she seemed young and vigorous—
Some queen of doubtful lineage to serve
This hive desperate to thrive *queenright* again.

Terzanelle with Lines from Bhartrihari

Renunciation of worldly attachment
is only the talk of scholars,
whose mouths are wordy with wisdom.

Renouncing, finally, all the world offers,
You put your hair back up. I watch you dress—
But isn't this only "the talk of scholars,"

Mouths "wordy with wisdom," who impress
Each other, but not us, with vague abstractions?
I touch your hair, gently, watching you dress,

Clasp pressed beside breast-shadow, all your actions
Well-timed and precise. Lovers grown tired
Of one another—not us—seek abstractions

Sometimes, reasons why they might feel scared,
Or trapped, or simply restless, all the nights,
So well-timed and precise, leaving them tired

Instead of touched with light, twin satellites
That separate at last. You find your skirt
Adrift beneath a chair, near crushed, the night's

Gains changed to loss. You look a little hurt,
Renouncing, finally, all the world offers,
More pain or pleasure, smoothing down your skirt,
Remembering, at most, the talk of scholars.

Strange Creature

After the Exeter Book's Riddle 29

Strange creature, soaring like a ship
That bears away its plunder, eyes
And features scissor-sharp, you light

Your own way in the sky, so deep
The darkness that surrounds you. Keep
Yourself concealed by day, silver

No stronghold can protect those hours
You round the world in shadow, but
By night put on your webs, your veils,

And while sleep still escapes you, search
The sky for one in hot pursuit,
Masked one who hides by night. Forsake

Once more your darker space, this sky
So deep that you could drown in it,
And disappear from view, quickly,

Before your body's taken . . . if
That's what you want, impatient one,
Strange creature now invisible.

Dante's Beatrice

Canto II

How long has she been dead, how many years
Raised to the light, set down among the saints
Confiding in each other as in life
About—what else?—a man who needs their help
More than he knows. And in the world below,
Despite the dark wood, "bitter, almost, as death,"
His life half over, if he's fortunate,
Dante constructs his Beatrice as she may—
No, *must* be—now that he is most in need:
"Blessed and beautiful" (she always was)
But more: a soul who turns when Lucy asks,
"Why won't you help him? Don't you hear his cries?"
Then listens past the music of the spheres—
That slow, celestial humming—for his voice.

Three Enchantments

1. *Scapular*

> *For Roman Catholics, a pair of small cloth squares*
> *depicting saints, the Sacred Heart, religious mottos, etc.*
> *worn around the neck for blessing or protection*

This is the real thing: two stamp-sized pictures
Mounted against brown felt, dangled from string
(Or surplus sneaker-lace?) to form a necklace
Worn to grant safe conduct through the fires
Of Hell, or Grief? Uncertain. Maybe both.
Here is "Our Queen" at Fatima, fiery heart
Displayed—white-veiled, haloed, arms spread wide—
Whoever dies wearing this scapular . . .
A motto meant to calm us. But it's the second
Image that hits home: a pair of hearts
Skewered on one sword, shredded, scratched by thorns,
Fire-seared, blood-smeared, yet bound together still—
Combustible, tortured heart, and tattered heart,
How can you now *Protect Us* with your light?

2. *Novena*

> *"Powerful Novena of Childlike Confidence";*
> *Imprimatur, January 2, 1942, New York*

What's left to try? And so we turn to these
Few words, this spell our parents vowed would work,
Daughters and sons who placed their trust in *prayers*
Invoked with "Childlike Confidence" to Christ,
Infant of Prague, red-robed: from child to Child.
Our last resort, when we could still believe,
And so again: once every hour, for nine,
We'll speak as we're required, make our request

Three times, pained by some blank space in our lives,
And then we'll wait, see what the waiting proves . . .
Does this Novena's "Power" derive from words,
Or from the one who hears it? Or from both?
Belief itself, perhaps: that it *has* power,
Belief in one who listens, one who saves.

3. *To Marie Laveau, on Opening Her Pamphlet*
   Her text includes the ritual approaches required of petitioners,
   as well as Laveau's spells and remarks on human nature

Oh, Good Mother, I come to you for help—
So all the spells begin, all true attempts
To gain advantage, finally, over fortune
Through applied belief. Oils of Verbena
And Rosemary—slowly stirred together,
Scrubbed into the walls—will call her home.
There should I wait, sprinkling on every floor
The Gold Magnetic Sand her feet will touch
The moment she arrives . . . *Marie Laveau,*
Whose pamphlet teaches much, when will she come?
—"I cannot say," she writes. "And yet, my son,
You most should read these words, and trust their power:
For love is at the bottom of all things,
The core of what we are, and rules the world."

A Way to Light

One window: one light shining in the dark
Devouring the many-storied building
Blacking out the stars, as I turn back
To view my own room—everything arranged
As it should—no, it *must* be—in a light
Dying of thirst tonight as time runs down
To its own breaking point, and I stay up
Long past the need for sleep, or for forgiveness.
This is it: how one room on some floor
Close to the sky can rise, or seem to rise,
Weightless, above wet streets, slack power lines,
Dead space, black slots of darkened rooms, dark lives
I'll never know, gold window that now holds—
Who'll say that it does not?—a way to light.

III

I admit the briar
Entangled in my hair
Did not injure me;
My blenching and trembling
Nothing but dissembling,
Nothing but coquetry.

— W. B. Yeats

I won't let bitterness quench my thirst—
and you shouldn't either.

— Edward Hirsch

Invocation

Muses, can it be true that you are one
Pure dazzling light of mind and spirit bent
On song and song alone, that one you love
Will find, in song, long-sought forgetfulness
As long as he keeps singing? To forget
Is all that I ask now: to feel this grief
Fall off, to lose all dark thoughts, to erase
The past, to keep on singing till her voice
Is lost, submerged in mine, to sing till song
Itself is all that's left, pure sound, this note
Raised from the throat, pure heartbeat, pulse of blood
In flesh, rhythm of breath, the world erased
But for one truth, one promise: to forget,
And so, begin again? I cannot stop.

Dante Alone

Canto I

Having lost heart but struggling to ascend
This steep road, shattered rock and wilderness
Creeping across his path, he stops at last
To find himself faced down by what he fears—
Leopard or lion, a wolf more ravenous
The more she's fed, eyes gleaming while she stares
Him down, scratching at gravel with her paws,
Circling before him restlessly. Not lost;
Guarding her place. Unmoved. She'll strike unless
He backs down now—one way that this could end.
And yet, half-turned toward darkness but before
He glimpses Virgil's ghost, pale bodyguard
And guide along this quest, *To be devoured,*
He thinks, *is better than to climb once more.*

Aristaeus Forgiven

Eurydice died . . .

That's where it often begins,
but remember how she died, the adder's bite
as she fled headlong from the lecherous

Aristaeus,
the cause of it all, or, less clear-cut than that,
mixed up somehow in the causes, part of them . . .
— Virgil, *Georgics*, IV, David R. Slavitt, translator

I'd watched Eurydice, bees edging near
The bouquet as she reached out, shooed them off
And stepped back, laughing, steadied by her bridesmaids,
Meadow in bloom, fierce humming underfoot
And overhead, snake unseen till it struck
—Such grief. Was I the cause? Desire repressed,
I'd watched her from a grove but stood revealed
Only when it was too late, angry swarm
Confusing everyone, those panicked women,
Spirits of wood and water, shrieking out
Despair and accusations as I fled—
Could they be right? I wondered: had I called
The bees to act as I could not, an impulse
Toward destruction—*tear the veil away*—
Still unacknowledged as I rose to witness—
Cause the tragedy? And when my bees,
Queenless themselves, mere husks, were dying off
In waves, I should have known my luck had turned
Against me for good reason: secretly,
The angry women watched, waiting their turn,
A grief for a grief, while time and fortune brought
Vengeance against the uninvited guest,
Bridesmaids-in-mourning loyal to the end.
What had I done, or not done? I'd forgotten,
Or fought back the thought, till Proteus
Reminded me. I flinched, but let him speak,
Tale garbled in the telling and retelling,

As I heard the rites that would appease
Mistaken enemies, though in my rage
I'm sure in time I would have sought the bulls
And heifers anyway, slaughtered them all,
And left them gutted somewhere, fury quenched
And vision darkened. *So this is forgiveness*,
I thought bitterly before the altar,
Newly purified . . . .

                But when I placed
My hand inside the carcass where new bees
Had gathered in the wound, and felt the nectar
Oozing at my touch, I had to laugh
At such grotesque fulfillment of my prayers,
False respite, restoration that meant less
Than full forgiveness. No, my guilt would last
As long as flesh—grief, too—and more would follow
In the years to come, stung hand recoiling,
Sticky with gold, defiled, a bridesmaid's laughter
Almost audible, sun streaming down
On bloodied altar, carcass, living bees
And empty meadow, all the years ahead.

Lives of the Sleepers

Some say they were three,
The dog being the fourth
Among them; others say
They were five, the dog
Being the sixth,—doubtfully
Guessing at the unknown;
Yet others say they were
Seven, the dog being the eighth.
                    . . . Enter not,
Therefore, into controversies
Concerning them . . .
                    — The Qur'an

I woke up. What I saw first was the light
On cave-walls, hardly light at all, a darkness
Not as deep, perhaps, now visible
Just past slicked-down stalactites. Then the dog
Katmir licking my hand. I lay still, listening—
How long had I slept?—sat up at last,
The stale air so damp I almost choked
To breathe too deeply. There it was, the light,
Surely a light toward which I rose, or stumbled,
Past those sleeping forms—*Malchus, Maximian,*
Which are you? I heard their breathing, shapes
I stepped past carefully, the dog's tail whacking
Loudly as they stirred. But when I reached
The passage out, alone, still wondering when

Centurions would find us, eyes cast down
I gave thanks anyway, dreamed voices nearly
Shaken off . . . World in light, a broken wall
Mortared to rock, now crumbling, and a space,
Man-sized, through which I squeezed. Dog-barks, a stream
Of wings toward sky, bird-shrieks and so much green
The world seemed painted. Emperor, if you
Can hear me now, why did you seal us up,

Decius, image embossed in coins I spent
Only too gladly? When we'd fled from you,
Our homes still under watch, looted, or burned
To rubble, friends gone cold, families afraid
For us and for themselves, I smashed your face
Between two rocks, screaming till Constantine

Grabbed hold to calm me down: a profile scratched
And dented, coin still chipped, I found, somehow,
Back in my tunic, with some likenesses
Undamaged, only—yes, another clue—
So black I hardly knew you, years of tarnish
Having done their work. How long? The road
Ran steeply downhill, cracked, clotted with weeds,
Covered with broken rocks, while Katmir rushed
Ahead, barking at trees, or gnawed on sticks,
Growling, and then caught up.
                                        A girl's face
Turned from me, talking steadily, soft words,
Some type of blessing, meaningless, but spoken
With such feeling while I stroked her hair
That I believed—
                                I knew her then, awake,

But could not search for her until I'd found
Some bread for my companions, rock-hard crumbs
All that was left when, on his hands and knees,
Marcian found his sack between stalagmites
Risen overnight. I saw the gates
Unguarded now, surprisingly, beneath
Thickets I hadn't seen before—a trap,
Or some small carelessness?—stalking through woods
Along the road, Katmir some yards ahead,
Sniffing the wall. We slipped into Ephesus
Where I'd find some friends, or partisans
To help us with supplies, and where I'd glimpse
Her briefly, if God willed it. Casually
I made my move, walked out where I could blend

Into the crowd at market, found a stall
Amid the vendors' noise, more cries, stripped meat
Revolving on a spit, and paid the baker,
With that face I hated, multiplied.
He paused, and for the first time, I looked up,
Afraid he'd recognized me, saw at once
The whole crowd staring back, people I knew
Not quite by name, dressed in such clothes I'd never
Seen before. Had we been moved, asleep,
Carried to some strange country? When I saw
Them bless themselves, I *knew*. Nothing that God
Wills ever should surprise us, yet I felt
Frightened, not grateful, furious at the thought
Of all those lost years—centuries, said some,

Handing my coins around, pulling the cross
Taut from my neck, and pointing, thanking God
As, right then, I could not. Hands dug in loaves,
I turned, Katmir behind me, barking back
The mob that hoped to follow. Scrapian
Most pious, who believes in miracles,
And now has seen one, what should I have done?
I wept, forcing my way back through the woods,
Face jabbed by branches, bleeding, now in flight
From Christians like myself, this bitter trade—
A lifetime for a world—not yet enough
To cancel out the loss, to know her voice
Is gone for all time, everyone I loved
Long dead. Until the Last Day. Or, as John

Would say, *Here is the patience of the saints*
Who keep the Lord's commandments. Every one . . .
I called before the cave, "Katmir, come here,"
A crescent moon just risen, broken sun
Red-orange at dusk. Crushed bread, a mortared wall
Crumbling . . . I faced a darkness where my friends
Survived, struggling awake, believing still
Their loved ones waited for them, no despair

Risen to break their faith.
                              As for her voice,
A music I could not shut out but hear
Even today, in sleep, my only prayer
Was that it would grow faint enough to bear
As, through the years, it has.
                              In light and air,
        As long as possible, I waited there.

In Assisi

St. Francis installed Clare and, later, her sister and
widowed mother as "the nucleus of a community in
a house by the Church of San Damiano at Assisi . . .
and this was the beginning of the order of Poor Ladies . . . "
— from Donald Attwater's *A Dictionary of Saints*

St. Clare, I've read, gave up her life to God,
Though just as stubbornly she meant to flee
Her family's hold for Francis of Assisi,
Charismatic preacher strangely proud
Of his own poverty. Only eighteen—
Impressionable, it seems—she heard his words
Declaimed with such conviction, as the Lord's
Prayer followed from his lips, surely no man
But he could satisfy her spirit's need
Fused, as it was, with flesh. Concealed by nuns,
She cut all ties beneath his gaze, but once
She took the lodgings offered her (Godspeed
To all Poor Clares), could she foresee the tears?
She outlived him by twenty-seven years.

Folly Bridge

Still she haunts me, phantomwise . . .
— from Lewis Carroll's dedicatory acrostic
in *Through the Looking-Glass*

From Folly Bridge to Nuneham, down the Isis,
Stroke and bow, oars raised, sun overhead,
Gull-shadows passing over, no rain yet
Despite the clouds, we pushed on, sudden wake
That caught us laughing. Coxswain of the boat,
I sat, Thames-water broken, fused again,
Damp woods and picnic huts our destination
Gliding into view. I'd find this day
Transformed—*The Pool of Tears, A Caucus-Race
And a Long Tale*—in the Wonderland he hadn't
Yet imagined, improvised aloud,
Or set down at my urging, sisters changed
To birds, Lory and Eaglet, Duckworth beaked,
Feathered to fit his name, himself revived
From long extinction, stammering once more,
Still soaked, Dod'son the Dodo, I alone,
Enlarged or miniaturized, myself, at least,
Storm-tossed in my own tears. I didn't know
That day was the beginning of the end,
That when we next met, course reversed to Godstow,
Basket of cakes, cold chicken, parasols
Throwing no shade, three sisters calling for
A story, *I* would fall, dim rabbit-tunnel
Beckoning, stroke and bow, past Oxford shops,
Groaning of oars, goose-calls, haze that pushed back
The world on shore still further, while I hung
On every word, his voice . . . Yes, I was lost—
We all were—borne upriver by the current—
What would happen next? His stammer gone,
As always, when he rowed, his face relaxed,
He spoke as one who'd found the tale complete,
Engraved in memory, and now reported

Back at leisure, calmly, coaxed to laugh
Whenever I broke in. We docked, and ate.
Pooled tears—more his than mine. For years we'd met
Within his rooms at Christ Church, drawn to puns
Or caricatures, self-portrait of a scholar
Frightened of class, till polishing the glass
Plate, joking while he worked, he'd disappear
Beneath black cloth, his "folding box of rosewood"
Balanced on its tripod, staring back.
"Hold absolutely still." Breath held, we'd wait,
Daughters of Dean Liddell, for hours turned over
To the deacon's care, then photographed,
Three Graces on a sofa. Once, he asked
Me to change clothes, excused himself to set
Up in the garden; thumping down the stairs,
I joined him outside, costumed in the rags
He'd brought, a beggar-child, palm out, to lean
Against the wall, clear-eyed and skeptical,
I'm told, an actress born. Later, face flushed
With anger at the pose I'd struck, my mother
Praised his eye—he understood, and left—
As she turned back and glared, "How dare he; you,
Of all to dress in such clothes; did he watch
You, help you get undressed . . . " I shook my head.
Could she mean Mr. Dod'son? I can see him,
Even now: black tie, starched collar, brown hair
Scarcely tamed, eyes creasing when he smiled
Or forced a smile; a sad face; overall,
A kind one . . . *Cheerfully, the crocodile*
Grins back, neatly spreads his jaws in welcome . . .
No, those aren't the right words: not one cut,
Body inviolate, I fell past miles
Of books but landed safely in a world
Of paradox and petty bickering.
We broke with him. Saddened, I held the book,
His first, handwritten version—delicate,
All dense calligraphy and careful drawings,
Frail illuminations, red and black,
To mark each chapter—after we'd cut off

All but required contact: hard at first,
Then easier, our mother having long
Foretold that we'd outgrow him. Even so,
I missed him for a few months, hoped he'd call,
But knew that when he did, I'd find myself
Distracted, glancing at the clock not for
Some puzzle in its numbers but because—
Admit it—I was bored. He talked so much!
Now that I saw him as he was—impoverished,
Fond of toys, touchy, obsessed with nonsense,
Charming, yes, but most at ease alone,
With a peculiar talent—I could not
Un-see what I had glimpsed. *Alas! Too late.*
She went on growing but ran out of room . . .
And afterward, the gossip—"Dod'son's gone
To pieces having found himself refused"—
But who could waste years on some long engagement
Under escort, made to look for guidance
From a fiancé so childish?
Six more years passed. When *Looking Glass* appeared,
Bound volumes in a bookshop window splashed
By carriages, I found myself surprised,
Compelled to look, the girl's face in a mirror
Half-immersed. I flipped through to the end—
Just as I feared: a poem. Worse, an acrostic,
ALICE PLEASANCE LIDDELL along the margin
Of melancholy lines, as if to grow
Up were to die—bright page, shop-door flung open,
Street-calls, harness-bells, crack of a whip
Abruptly muffled. I set down the book,
And felt . . . never more certain. He'd no right
To claim such grief—and yet, I understood:
For all his kindnesses, he'd fallen short
Of some ideal departure when he lost
My "willing ear," he called it in his poem,
Ashamed not to have seen how false his hope
Had always been, worse yet to have foreseen,
And forged ahead, sums changed to differences,
Wit and armor shed . . . *'Once you've crossed*

To the next brook,' said the Knight, 'I'll see you safe
Up to the woods' edge. Then I'll have to leave—
You know, it's where my move ends.' So it goes:
Loss, victory, or draw, it's all the same.
When Edith died at twenty-two, a bride-
To-be, engaged to Nuneham's heir, I lost
A sister and all hope. My own true prince
Bled at the slightest wound (a kindred spirit,
You'd have found), though what drove us apart
Was not affliction but a Queen's decree,
Long-planned maneuverings. What else was left?
Assent to Mr. Hargreaves and a house,
Well staffed, to organize, three sons to bear,
An absent husband, noise and emptiness,
While you, recovered finally, still prospered
In your work, an alter ego's fame,
New child-friends and new photographs more daring
Than the ones we shared. You died before
The century's turn, but I've lived long enough
To see our world disappear, faint glow
Beyond the far banks, oars raised, two sons killed
In the Great War. Yes, some griefs are worse than love's
Mere accidents. Could there have been a time
When all that lay before us was a land
Of wonder, limitless imaginings
Still to be given voice? You wrote in courtship,
Mr. Dod'son, borne up by a faith
Near-childlike in its certainty that words
Would resurrect a girl, a time and place,
Oar-splash along the Isis, given up
To depths unknown when we set off that day.

Ophelia: A Wreath

Water like glass unbroken, silent stream,
Or almost so; broad willow-branch in shadow,
Crowflowers, nettles, columbines, a dream

Of freedom: fish that vanish in mid-gleam
Close to the surface. Grief above, below
Water like glass unbroken, silent stream

Of glitterings, sky-fallings. Whispered name,
Words sung, snatches of nonsense. Listen now:
Crowflowers, nettles, columbines, a dream

Where every garland flares up into flame—
Blood-red, black-purple. *Where should this one go?*
Water like glass unbroken, silent stream

Into—what next? Stained palms, cathedral-dome
Of sun blinding beyond high branches. Show
Us crowflowers, nettles, columbines, a dream—

Glass shattering, wreath-drenched. Silence the same
As singing? Hair unravelling, undertow . . .
Water like glass. Unbroken, silent stream
Of crowflowers, nettles, columbines. A dream.

Cycles of Catastrophe in Petrarch

Six centuries after his trials and tribulations ended,
the poetic pieces of Petrarch's emotional jigsaw
begin to fall into place at last, with the help of
catastrophe theory. Who knows how many other
streams of love-lyrics from the past could be
disentangled with similar kinds of mathematical
thinking?

— Frederic Jones, on the structure
of Petrarch's *Canzoniere*

A girl beneath green laurel I remember,
White as ivory, colder than snow untouched
Or so she seems, transformed in memory,
To metaphor, ideal. What lies behind
The poet's art and craft—catastrophe,
And two real people: Petrarch, scholar-laureate
Of an empire's fragment, drawn to Laura,
Living woman, muse—some theorists use
The "cusp equation" to identify.
With Petrarch cast as *x*, Laura as *y*,
The poet sees her first—off-limits, married—
Praying at Saint Clare's chapel. Now the flood
Begins: twenty-one years   *From me you've seized*
All power to desire, or end desire

A lifetime's worth of poems that won't slow down
Till Plague takes Laura, most of Avignon.
The cycle starts with kindness—Laura's voice
A mild rebuke that gives rise to false hope
That spurs you, Petrarch, to write poems, swear oaths
Of friendship, pure Platonic fealty
You'll shatter, reaching the cusp at new extremes
Of ecstasy or loss: abrupt collision,
Impact   *"What if I weren't what you think?"*
She dares say—quantum leap from love to pain—

A math past calculus. Now "splitting factors"
Grip you: pure will met by pure resolve,
She turns back your advances. Laura, why stop
To read at all, as if to test yourself

Against his eloquence, this papal courier
Whose true aim is clear? This latest cycle
Soon commences in a quiet phase:
You nudge him gently—forward, not away.
She walks: her footsteps on the river's edge
Tamp down wet grass, the slenderness of trees
Around her like her own, half-light where sun
Breaks into gold smoke   Hard to turn away
From such words—plus, you recognize yourself.
And yet, who wouldn't look, spatter of wax
Across the page, flame doused, a voice set down
And shut away before your husband sees?
What if you'd never wed—if you were widowed?
What else would you lose? And so, you choose

Contact, such as it is, with one who'll find
More, always, than you meant by any faint
Smile, glance, or offhand word, at the expense
Of solitude, or peace.   *Yes, I've come near*
The end, at times, but after all these years,
What's left? I've come now to depend on grief,
To cause it, seek it out   Is this the voice
Of a changed man? Still, rejection takes its toll:
He learns, through many setbacks, to provoke
Fury or sympathy, gauging the risk
To you and to himself, a more restrictive
Cycle better modelled by the so-called
"Butterfly equation": here, a fleeting
Equilibrium is reached, eruptions

Choked back or, at least, better concealed.
The wind that turns its back on her bright plumage
Wastes its words on air   But this won't last.
More drastic metaphors will soon explode
This calm that isn't calm, this passing mood.
Still, if we plot each outburst and retreat—
The axes are Emotion versus Time—
As we might graph other phenomena
(Rivers in flood, whirlpools), what forms emerge?
A sine curve: jagged peaks and sudden depths—
In short, catastrophes   *Arise, and fall,*
Despair or bliss, I thrive on both alike
And cutting past the diagram's steep swirls,
A clear "forbidden zone" that neither enters:

Unforced friendship, calm, mutual love—
I'm still the one I was. I haven't moved
I want to ask: did writing poems extend
The cycles past their natural end? What act
Of will sustained you, Petrarch, through the years
Your pleas went unfulfilled? When did you know
Your life's work had been founded on the prospect
That you'd be denied? Laura, was life
For you more than two decades of refusals,
And a swift decline? Did you forgive
The poet his wrongs, his art and self-deceptions?
Sorrow creates strange shapes. I laugh and sing
Because I have no other hiding place
There's no equation, yet, to tell us so.

Desire: A Bestiary

Banana Slug

Banana slugs—*dolichophallus,*
named for what they look like,
partly for what they possess—
are hermaphrodites. Their yellow flesh
glistening on the ground
invites pursuit, a slime-trail traced
till chaser overtakes the chased,
who shrinks from the touch of radulae,
turns back, reciprocates.
But which, at last, will "dominate"?

Flesh is muscle to be flexed.
What happens next? Only what must:
slow thrashing, mutual response—
the point and counterpoint of all.
Even so, the third day ends
with one last act of appetite,
when "she" devours all difference,
gnawing while her partner bends
to share the same flesh: it's his *name*
they feed upon.

Denouement

One doesn't often get a second chance. I want to stop being haunted.
— John "Scot" Ferguson (Jimmy Stewart) to "Madeleine
Elster"/ "Carlotta Valdes"/Judy Barton (Kim Novak)
in Alfred Hitchcock's *Vertigo*, 1958

The bell-tower closes in. It ends at last
With one more forced ascent, bleached hair, black dress
And borrowed necklace, keepsake of a past
That haunts you both: a "made-to-order witness"
Helpless to act, guilt-wracked, bound for the top,
And one poor Kansas girl made over twice,
This time reluctantly, desperate to please
At any cost, steep drop,
Small chance of breaking free. Lies within lies—
She fears your tightening hold, or its release,

Your rage, these accusations. "This was as far
As I could get," you snarl, the stairs that led
Her from you, straight ahead. More than a year
Ago, you saw her die—
              But was *she dead?*
Or had you glimpsed a stranger's plunge through light,
Dead wife pushed out on cue? You heard the live
Imposter scream—all you could do was watch,
Frozen at such a height,
Trembling in place, in love, left to survive,
Failed guardian, false memory of touch

Your only recompense. And in the shadow
Of the bell, still hidden, Elster's hand
Clasped on your lover's mouth . . .
                    Why tell her now
You've finally got it figured out, grave opened,
"Clean and waiting"—weren't those her words?—
Last, deep plunge into nothingness, or all
You'd ever hoped? Each twist unfurled, hair down,
And you're still shouting, chords

71

Struck harshly as you climb, sharp cries, kicked heel
And slap ignored, missed step past mortared stone

And plaster—till, a few steps from the belfry,
You exult, "I made it," though the ghost
Before you—not yet exorcised, exactly
As she looked before, except more lost,
Near tears, caught on this last flight—flees your grasp
Instead of seeking it. What can you say
To close this reckoning? Just one more floor,
And you'll be free, locked clasp
And coiled bouquet discarded, seething Bay
Beneath the Golden Gate, thick breaths of air

You'll gulp down greedily.
                            But when you force
Her once more to the crime scene, arms pulled taut
Despite her shrieks, concocted family curse
Long buried with "Carlotta," careful shot
Of tarnished bell, forged brass a century old,
You'll hesitate . . . What sort of world surrounds
You?
    Broken thread of coastline, whirling view
From which all truth's withheld,
Dead-ends in close-cropped greenery, choked sounds
And more recriminations, pleas for you

To stop, have mercy . . .
                       Nothing is enough:
You'll never *know*, though you'll insist she listen
To a full accounting, battered cliff
Assaulting memory, the ghost's possession
Forfeited, no chance to recreate
Her trance or your belief, before this kiss
You'll fail to consummate. Too late. Escape's
Impossible, her fate
Long foreordained, like yours: to fall. Your face
Tells everything: dead heart where nothing leaps.

Recantation

Time to recant: as if this world of ice
Survives unchanged from some primeval time
Still cut off from the mainland. So much ice—
Ground down by wind and snow, in storms of ice
Nearly unending, clear walls that divide
Us both, eroded caves, this crumbling ice
Like smashed glass in gloved hands. An Arctic ice,
Miles thick, blurred shadows trapped inside, a life
Cut off, time stopped, the isotope's half-life
Measuring loss, what's captured in scratched ice
Within our reach, yet far away. But why?
It's time. Take it all back. I once knew why

I woke in sunlight, cold, afraid of why
The wind seared through, a straight line over ice
Groaning beneath blue sky. I won't ask why,
Or where you disappeared. Look at these white
Cliffs, palisades of ice: we're lost in time,
Great temblors, bodies fossilized, smashed Y
Of pelvis, cloudy fur. I don't know why
You left. Take back the words, the acts. Divide
Our trails, snow-filled in minutes, or divide
Millennia from the present: tell me why
You fade in snow, erased . . . Around us, life
Exists—microbial, sunk in ice, brief life

On hold, freeze-frame in darkness, afterlife
Some interglacial thaw? I look for *why*—
The chromosomal alphabet, past lives,
Or lovers intertwined, helix of life . . .
Let go. Unravel now. Nothing our eyes
See can be un-seen, axis charged with life,
Aurora flashing, words forged to outlive
Their telling, none erased, while over time
Ice melts, and water churns to ice. In time
Will we still have a choice? Why look for life
In wastes so frozen cells cannot divide?
I look back: sky far off, our long divide

From eons past, tectonic plates dividing
Ice-sheets, continents. What is a life
Except more years to watch ourselves divide
One from another, helplessly? Divide
Days from extended nights, the reasons why
Ice gleams or darkens. Nothing we divide
Is ever whole again: recant. Divide
This bread from broken flesh, one heart of ice
Imploding while I face these walls of ice
Enclosing all. What frozen lake divides
Us from the world above? And how much time
Is *for all time?* Back in some other time,

Near dusk, crossing a river, wintertime,
I stopped, looked down to see how ice divides
Reflections from a world, smudged trees and time
Looming below, without end. Out of time,
Walking on soundless ice, I see no life
Except these shadows hovering, lifetimes
Used up, some clasped together, all held timeless,
Lost at different depths. If I asked why
They flail in ice, submerged, bodies bleached white,
What could they say, imprisoned for all time,
But lucky, too—nothing to say that ice
Won't silence—staring upward, eyes of ice,

An anguish beyond pain. *Not locked in ice*
But waiting for our moment, for the time
To take back all we've lived, though ice divides
Us from forgiveness and another life—
We're shattered glass. Gather us carefully.

Two Departures

Once, when you turned and waved,
Hair flashing on your shoulder
As through a crowd you moved
Boarding the plane, I waved,
Turning, at last, away. I loved
Your every word and gesture
Once, when you turned and waved,
Hair falling on your shoulder.

Nothing I could observe
Prepared me for your turning,
Letting a cool reserve
(All that I dared observe)
Follow the plane's bright curve
Deadening into morning . . .
Nothing I dared observe
Woke me to what was turning

Into a grief, long absence
Fallen like snow in sleep . . .
If, after weeks of silence
Much like a final absence,
You could return—but, once,
You did, which is why I keep
Hold of this grief, your absence
Troubling me in sleep.

How can you stand the silence?
What will return in sleep?
World without sense or balance
Lost at the train, in silence . . .
Late to a station, tense
With waiting, the tunnel deep,
Smiling, you turned in silence
Both of us now will keep.

Desire: A Bestiary

Slipper Limpet

A periwinkle, limpet-shaped,
crepidula fornicata
undergoes transfiguration,
change of gender, resignation,
having settled on a rock.
A newly minted female
fitted for the passing shell
of what she was, she clings for life
till a former self slips over,
firmly locks himself in place
till another lands on *him*—
soon, *he* is *she*—and still
one more, accommodating
each new partner
in the chain, the one before
(each shoe a foot, a shoe once more),
shells gathered in a heap,
a female anchored at its base,
others in metamorphosis,
one lone male at the top. When,
if ever, does it stop? When
one *breaks* the chain?
When some force splits apart
shell fused to shell? But in
the meantime, so much patience,
deference to the common good, impulse
alive in order, certainty
in change.

Expectation of a Journey

You can follow us, but you cannot stay here and follow us.
— Marshall Herff Applewhite
(known to his flock as "Do")

Dust of deep space, radiant heat, a trail,
Bright sphere vaporized, wandering star
Frozen at the horizon, our conveyance
Hidden behind your light, when will we leave
These bodies, such poor vehicles? Not now,
But soon . . .
　　　　　　　We take our places, aching legs
Crossed lotus-style, a garden overrun,
The telescope arched skyward. Eyes still bright,
We gaze at Hale-Bopp, the pre-dawn palms
Ruffled by wind, pool gleaming, on the grounds
Of one more rented mansion in a world
Too dark to read, the Great Do gaunt and speechless,
Peering through his binoculars, all-wise
Conductor of the choir that is our lives.
A week ago, turning from my computer,
I saw light—clean water, chlorine-blue—
A piece of sky held, rippling, in cement,
Place to submerge or plummet to the sound
Of keyboards pounding furiously. Between
This world of light, bright window, and this screen,
Postmodern icons flashing from a page
Still only half-constructed, I escaped,
Logged out to surf the Net, found your address,
Then acted on my own: guessed today's password,
Typed, *I know my life might puzzle you—*
But how can I explain?—e-mailed at last,
Deleting swiftly, precious time I owed
Great Do, my brothers, sisters, and the Ones
Who wait beyond Hale-Bopp.
　　　　　　　　　　　I'd sinned before,

But this was worse: sin cubed, a secret kept
Beyond a day, sent to the Outside World
To one I shouldn't still love.
                                        Then the screen
Blossomed back into fragments, stars on fire
Swirling in clusters, galaxies on black.
Our leader's merciful. He gave me time,
Three full days to come forward on my own,
And yet I didn't. Who had I become—
Next Level Crewman ready to ascend,
Earthly container shed, or still the same
Small boy who cowered from his parents' rage?
Whatever I was, I waited. Then a brother
Touched my arm, and I knew I was caught.
With bursts of whale-song piping through the halls,
I listened, knocked twice, found myself called in
To face Do's gaze, clean light, each cadence struck
Gently: "My poor lost lamb." He spoke of Ti,
Note nearest to his own, whose voice he heard
Through the celestial sphere, still guiding him—
Even today, long dead? "No. Disappeared.
What was it like for her?" he asked, then offered,
"Not death but a passing: as if Someone
Touched the door, set free the passenger
Inside to shop for some new vehicle
Bright gold and supercharged, full tank of gas,
A star-map on the driver's seat." They spoke—
Yes, spoke—despite the silence deep space held,
Despite black holes that feed on galaxies,
Two voices, Ti and Do. I'd only meant,
Like him, to send words rippling through the void
Of cyberspace, to justify, explain—
Do raised his hand. "But Ti was one of *us*.
Enlightened." Yes. Of course: the crucial difference.
Bottle in hand, pure alpine water flashing
As he drank, he swivelled his chair, to gaze
Out, tranquil, toward that other life I'd sought
And nearly sacrificed—for whom? Ashamed,
I wept, excused from punishment, from harm,

Grateful, again, for all—our fellowship,
The surgery that cut out at the root
Those wrongful drives. . . .
                         New star that calls us forth,
Inverted streak, last brush-stroke; final stop
In Virgo where, one day soon, we'll all fly out,
One happy family headed for new lives.
That night, back in the fold, the T.V. bright,
I gasped when Do's dead ringer swooned, collapsed,
Bridge crew alarmed, while all the time he lay
Before them, struck down by some covert beam
Invisible to all, he glimpsed the life
He might have led, bliss to apocalypse,
While we looked on, transfixed, our hopes entrusted
To a gleaming starship.
                         Now, at dawn,
Deep blue blots out the stars, as Do lets fall
Binoculars, and beckons. . . . If you and I
Could pause as easily, fast forward to
The life we might have shared, light years condensed
To moments, would it be so wrong to try?

I wish that I could wait for your reply.

Field

These floodlights over the playing field glare
Through light rain—it's misting—and the drops,
Struck by the light, are swirling past the sky,
Slicked backdrop of the stands, the empty seats,
Soaked dugouts, wet grass, chalk lines trampled out
Or rained on, wiped away—sweeping across
Our field of vision, scattering in light,
Falling as more replace them, flashing now,
Charged mist pulled endlessly beyond the light,
Part of the light. We're walking far enough
Away to see the darkness that surrounds
This field's far from complete, though it holds us
—*Autumn in Baltimore. Still feels like summer*—
Part of a world that lies beyond the light.

First Thaw

This morning was the first time: all the snow
That buried us receding, still in drifts
Piled high, crusted with ice and yet receding,
Slowly drawing back—abandoned cars
Revealed, crushed grass, the shattered road ice-slicked,
Salt-splashed, slush running downstream, breaking up
Over the drains, dissolving . . . All this time
I thought the whole world lost, but now the light
Glances off roofs still cracking with the weight—
A little less, today. The second time
Is now: when I can bear to look around
Once more and watch this world emerge—old world
From which so much is missing still, new world
In which so much will, one day soon, appear.

House of Song

In Zoroastrian belief, those who live
a virtuous life are awarded paradise
in the "House of Song." The prince
is Gautama Buddha. The quotation
is from The Tibetan Book of the Dead.

After a long fast, long in solitude,
Footsore through burned-out fields, each like the next,
The Prince no longer recognized himself
When he bent down to drink, the dried blood caked
Across his face, cupped hands. What could he do
Just then but take the bowl—rice cooked in milk—
And thank the woman who stood over him
And offered *life*—there where the road ran out,
Bruised flesh too frail to bear him? So I choose
As well to rest here in a stranger's house,
Hosts absent for the week, rooms filled with light
For now, where I can thank this one I loved
For years and who now offers *life* again.
Last night, the two of us drove to the sea

Flashing on sand, slate-gray, the sky gone gray,
Late summer nightfall, kelp bunched under foot,
The night held back as if this were the *Time*
Between I'd read about—when I'll renounce
All that I knew and loved, including one
Who walked beside me then, her arm locked in
My own, as I'd renounced her once before.
For *you*—familiar tale. And laid before her
There, cracked shell of horseshoe crab, stone-smooth
Interior of whelk; sandpiper running
Toward the tide to be chased back again.
I laughed—*And still I saw you as you looked*—
Cheap plastic stereoscope bought at some beach
In Ocean City—held beyond the eyepiece:

Bodies struck by sun, you and your sisters
Smiling for the camera as the waves
Behind broke up, blue jewel-like surfaces
Frozen in mid-change, gleaming wet gold hair
—And then, headlights turned off, I drove her home,
"Our" house, for now. If it's ridiculous
To look for order in the grief we've caused
Ourselves and others, I'm just like the rest
Of us, all on the same search: like that Prince
Sealed off, somehow, from illness and from death,
Who glimpsed them for the first time on the day
He rode out from the palace, on the cushions
Of his chariot; who saw the corpse,
White-robed and pale, carried beyond the mourners

Weeping for the loss. Hard not to laugh
At someone who so missed the obvious
—Does he resemble us? And in that house
Pummeled by rain one whole day, while I slept
Or paged through books, she showered, sand in the hair
She towelled off, combed out, shook, black mane still wet,
Drops falling on my skin. Or fed the fish,
The cat, herself, and me, while all the glass
In every window shook, and rain poured down,
A storm, bed-tumblings, nightfall, then the rug,
White blanket stretched on knees, where she could read
By lamplight till the cat thumped to the floor.
The storm was over. Did I choose this house,
This time and place to heal the breach, this life

That bears us from the *Time Between* to *Now?*
"Hey, Noble One! If you cannot resist
Birth into suffering, call on the light
To guide you to a good womb"—
                                        To this bridge
Over the Charles, deep blue waves breaking down
To white shards as you laughed, a snapshot framed,
Your voice a scale ascending—

Lost the page.
Maybe the real blessing's to be born
Life after life until we get it right—
I get it right. Another chance. And if
Finally, those chances used up, I arrive
Within the House of Song, what will I find?
No pain, I've read—I don't know if there's joy—
And though I know the self will have been shattered

To a million pieces, all the world
Fused into one, its harmonies revealed,
The House that I imagine—infinite,
Made all of glass, trembling in one huge chord
Struck from all music—holds within its rooms
Each moment of *this* life, all those I've loved
Not yet gone from the earth, all those who are—
Each to survive for all time. Like the Prince
Who found the dawn-star flaring from the dark—
Enlightenment—alone, after a kindness,
I, too, want to live, to feel these moments
Here, alive within me, no one lost
From view, no voice gone silent, in this House—
This time, this world. No one I would refuse.

Amagansett, Long Island, August 1996

Desire: A Bestiary

Bonobo

In the rain forests of Zaire,
bonobos, their numbers dwindling,
grasp each other and hold close,
break away, and change position,
partner, angle of repose
—numbers fewer, despite coupling
for some part of every hour,
without violence
from the act's suggestion
to its aftermath, conflicts smoothed
through mutterings, a quick kiss,
squeeze or sudden touch—in their rapport,
closer than we are
to our common ancestor
(Wet with dusk, grasses tremble
from whose passage
at this hour?)
—Even the children drawn, as we are,
to all mysteries of touch,
those small acts surrounding
our creation.

A Star

For you, nothing but love,
All you desire to have
Restored as once before,
Even as all we were
Within the other's eye
Escapes us. Would you say
Love was the world to us?
Let us remember less
As if tonight a star
More steady than we are
Alone appears at last.
No need to say what's past—
Delight and memory
Are all you gave to me.

Notes

The poems comprising **Desire: A Bestiary** are drawn from the inspiration of Apollinaire and, more immediately, from the text and art of Dugald Stermer in his book, *Birds & Bees: A Sexual Study* (HarperCollins, 1995).

One source for **Lives of the Saints** is Reverend Lawrence G. Lovasik's *New Picture Book of Saints* (Catholic Book Publishing Company, 1979-1974-1962).

And as J. C. Perry and G. E. Vaillant remind us, many "saints, artists, revolutionary heroes, and true innovators" suffered from personality disorders (*Comprehensive Textbook of Psychology:* Williams and Wilkins, 1989).

In **After Hitchcock**, 1. and 2. are drawn from the film *Vertigo* (1958), 3. from *The Birds* (1964).

Blessing: Barbara Stoler Miller, translator of Bilhana's "Fantasies of a Love-Thief," writes, "According to legend, Bilhana became involved in a secret affair with the king's young daughter whom he was supposed to be instructing in the subtleties of literature . . ." From *The Hermit and the Love-Thief* (Penguin, 1990).

Millennial makes use of material from several articles, including the uncredited "Many Reports of Deformities Among Frogs Are Puzzling" (*New York Times*, October 13, 1996) and "Bad Days on the Lily Pad" (Sharon Begley with Thomas Hayden, *Newsweek*, July 13, 1998). Consulted also were Lawrence Wright's "Silent Sperm" (*The New Yorker*, January 15, 1996) and "Infant Named Hope, Born with Extra Limbs, Inspires as She Survives" (Knight Ridder News Service, *Baltimore Sun*, September 29, 1996). Italicized quotations are adapted from the books of Revelation, Exodus, and Leviticus.

Avalokitesvara is "a celestial Bodhisattva (a dedicated seeker of enlightenment) who is the archetype of universal compassion throughout the Buddhist world . . . [He] vowed that he would emanate as millions of Bodhisattvas *after* attaining the perfect enlightenment of Buddhahood, in order to stay close to suffering beings . . ." In traditional depictions, the god's ten heads and thousand arms indicate his willingness to reach out his saving hand to all who suffer. Robert A. F. Thurman, *The Tibetan Book of the Dead* (Bantam, 1994).

A meditation card which invokes the god includes this inscription: "The opening heart is the most beautiful flower of all."

Entries in the Dream Book: The book in question is *Understanding Dreams: A Concise Guide to Dream Symbols* (Running Press Book Publishers, 1994).

The epigraph in **Queenright** derives from Richard Bonney's *Hive Management* (Garden Way, 1990), which also provided the background information on bee-keeping practices.

Terzanelle with Lines from Bhartrihari: According to Barbara Stoler Miller, "Popular stories portray Bhartrihari as a world-weary king who renounced society in bitter reaction to the infidelity of lovers." The quoted lines appear in the last stanza of "Passionate Encounters," the second part of Bhartrihari's *Satakatraya* (included in the volume *The Hermit and the Love-Thief*).

Strange Creature: Kevin Crossley-Holland's note on the solution to Anglo-Saxon Exeter Book Riddle 29 reads, in part, "*Moon and sun* is widely accepted, although a case has also been made out for *swallow and sparrow, bird and wind,* and *cloud and wind.*" From *The Exeter Book Riddles* (Penguin, 1993).

In **Three Enchantments** the epigraph to "Novena" refers to the date and place when this particular ritualized prayer received official sanction from the Roman Catholic Church.

"To Marie Laveau, on Opening Her Pamphlet"—that is, *Old and New Black and White Magic: Burning of Candles, Use of Roots and Oils, Powders and Incense*; a publisher is not noted. Each spell includes the voice of the petitioner, as well as response and instructions in Laveau's own voice.

Aristaeus Forgiven draws on David R. Slavitt's translation of Georgica IV in *Eclogues & Georgics of Virgil* (Johns Hopkins, 1990). *Bulfinch's Mythology* (Random House) includes this summary of Proteus' words to Aristaeus: "You receive the merited award of your deeds, by which Eurydice met her death, for in flying from you she trod upon a serpent, of whose bite she died. To avenge her death, the nymphs, her companions, have sent this destruction to your bees. You have to appease their anger. . . . "

In addition to the Qur'an, sources for **Lives of the Sleepers** include the entry in Donald Attwater's *A Dictionary of Saints* (Penguin, 1975), as well as Sean Kelly and Rosemary Rogers' *Saints Preserve Us!* (Random House, 1993).

The unnamed sleeper, speaker of the poem, is Denis, though the sleepers' names vary considerably in different versions of the myth. In most accounts, however, the emperor sentences a group of Christians to death for their religious beliefs; they find shelter in a cave, fall asleep, and awake to a different world.

Sources for **Folly Bridge** include Lewis Carroll's *Alice's Adventures in Wonderland* and *Through the Looking-Glass;* additional information is drawn from Stephanie Lovett Stoffel's *Lewis Carroll in Wonderland* (Abrams, 1997), Christina Bjork and Inga-Karin Eriksson's *The Other Alice* (R & S Books, 1993), and from two articles on Morton Cohen's *Lewis Carroll: A Biography* (Knopf, 1995): Adam Gopnik's

"Wonderland" (*The New Yorker*, October 9, 1995) and Richard Jenkyns' "And Quiet Flows the Don" (*The New Republic*, January 29, 1996).

Cycles of Catastrophe in Petrarch adapts material from Frederic Jones' article "What's Catastrophe Got to Do with It?" (*New Scientist*, December 1994) and, very freely, from Petrarch's poems as translated by Nicholas Kilmer in *Songs and Sonnets from Laura's Lifetime* (North Point, 1981).

According to Jones, "The duration of the love affair was exactly 21 years between [Petrarch's] first meeting with Laura on Good Friday, 6 April 1327 and her death, almost certainly of the Black Death, on 6 April 1348." The cusp equation does not actually rely on x and y variables.

Expectation of a Journey: The Heaven's Gate cult members committed mass suicide inside a rented mansion in Rancho Santa Fe, California, during the three-day period immediately following the comet Hale-Bopp's closest approach to Earth (4 a.m., Saturday, March 22, 1997). In the 1960s Applewhite had been a college music professor and voice teacher, but from the 1970s on, he led several cults in collaboration with Bonnie Nettles ("Ti"), who died in 1985.

The group earned living expenses by designing Web pages, and the men were indeed castrated to encourage celibacy. Among the cult members' favorite television shows was *Star Trek: The Next Generation*, which they would watch as a community. References in the last stanzas are to the episode entitled "The Inner Light."

House of Song: In Peter Occhiogrosso's account of Zoroastrianism in *The Joy of Sects: A Spirited Guide to the World's Religious Traditions* (Doubleday, 1996), the existence of good and evil reflects events set in motion by Ahura Mazda, the world's creator: ". . . according to Zoroastrian cosmogony, one of the twin spirits engendered by Ahura Mazda, *Spenta Mainyu* ('Benificent Spirit') chose good and life, while the other, *Angra Mainyu* ('Destroying Spirit') . . . chose evil and death. As a result, mortals must make the same choice, and they will be judged accordingly upon their death, the just rewarded with entrance into paradise, or the 'House of Song,' the wicked condemned to the 'House of Evil.'"

The call, "Hey, Noble One!" appears in Robert Thurman's version of *The Tibetan Book of the Dead*.

About the Author

Ned Balbo grew up on Long Island, New York, and holds degrees from Vassar College, the Writing Seminars at Johns Hopkins, and the Iowa Writers' Workshop. He has received the Robert Frost Foundation Poetry Award and the John Guyon Literary Nonfiction Prize; his first collection, *Galileo's Banquet*, was awarded the 1998 Towson University Prize for Literature. He has been a Walter E. Dakin fellow in poetry at the Sewanee Writers' Conference, a National Italian-American Foundation fellow at the West Chester University Poetry Conference, and a poetry fellow at the Virginia Center for the Creative Arts. His reviews appear regularly in *Antioch Review* and *Pleiades*, and his poems have appeared in *American Poetry Review, Antioch Review, Crab Orchard Review, Die Cast Garden* (on-line), *The Formalist, Italian Americana, Notre Dame Review,* and elsewhere. He teaches at Loyola College in Baltimore.